The Gilded Age

ISBN-13: 978-0-15-352962-7
ISBN-10: 0-15-352962-8

1 2 3 4 5 6 7 8 9 10   179   13 12 11 10 09 08

Harcourt
SCHOOL PUBLISHERS

Visit *The Learning Site!* www.harcourtschool.com

The Rich Get Richer

One evening in 1903, a rich entrepreneur named C. K. Billings gave a very unusual dinner party. He was celebrating the building of a huge new stable for his racehorses. Billings invited 36 friends to a restaurant in New York City.

Fake grass covered the floor. The waiters wore the uniforms of grooms, or people who take care of horses. Guests climbed steps to reach their high seats—on horseback! Each horse's saddle was fitted with a special tray to hold plates and glasses.

This was one of many fancy parties held during the "Gilded Age" of the United States. As the country became an industrial nation, some people became very, very rich. They built huge mansions, collected art, and raised racehorses.

Parties could be quite fancy during the Gilded Age.

These people made their money in booming industries. They owned railroads, steel mills, oil companies, and banks. Billings, for example, had been the president of a gaslight company.

Some people called these men "robber barons." The name suggested that they had grown rich in dishonest ways. Many of them had. Other people called them "captains of industry" and considered them strong leaders. Many of them were.

The super-rich had more money than most Americans could even imagine. In the late 1800s, an average American made about $500 in a year. Andrew Carnegie, the owner of a steel company, made about $10 *million* each year!

The Gilded Age was a novel by Mark Twain and Charles Dudley Warner.

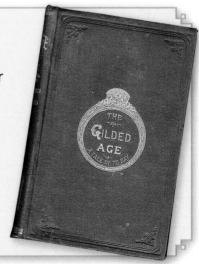

What's in a Name?

Gilded means "covered with a thin layer of gold." Something that is gilded may look like solid gold, but it is made of a cheaper metal under its shiny coating. People began using the phrase *Gilded Age*, from the title of a novel, to describe an era when appearances were more important than reality.

Mrs. Astor's 400

In the 1870s, Caroline Astor began a list of the top members of New York's high society. The list was called "Mrs. Astor's 400" or simply "the 400."

Caroline Astor

Why 400? One story says that 400 people could fit into Caroline Astor's ballroom in her Millionaires' Row mansion. In the winter of 1892, the *New York Times* printed the guest list for her February ball. People were very interested to see who was—and who was not—on the list.

The many balls and parties of the day were like events out of fairy tales. In March 1883, Alva and William Vanderbilt invited about 1,000 guests to a costume ball at their new mansion.

At the time it was built, Caroline Astor's home on Millionaires' Row was the grandest New York had ever seen.

Carriage after carriage pulled up to the entrance. Guests came dressed as famous people, such as Christopher Columbus, Daniel Boone, and Joan of Arc. One newspaper described the party as being "like a dream." Alva Vanderbilt dressed as an Italian princess in a fancy gown. Around her waist was a belt of pearls. Some of them had once belonged to the Empress of Russia.

The Empire State Building now stands on the site of the original Waldorf-Astoria.

The super-rich also traveled in luxury. They stayed in hotels that were as fancy as their mansions. One was the St. Regis, New York City's first skyscraper hotel. Another was the Waldorf Hotel, opened in 1893 by William Waldorf Astor. Four years later, his cousin, John Jacob Astor IV, built the Astoria Hotel next door. After a connecting passage was built, the two hotels became known as the Waldorf-Astoria.

Too Much Wealth?

Not everyone approved of all the wealth of the Gilded Age. In 1899, an economist named Thorstein Veblen wrote a book called *The Theory of the Leisure Class.* He described the lives of people who were so rich that they did not need to work. Veblen called things like a $15,000 dog collar examples of "conspicuous consumption." We still use this term; it means spending money on luxuries just to show how rich you are.

Millionaires' Row

As railroads, factories, and companies grew, neighborhoods changed. One stretch of Fifth Avenue in New York City went from being a bumpy dirt road to a street of magnificent mansions facing Central Park. People began to call this section of Fifth Avenue "Millionaires' Row" or "the Gold Coast."

The Vanderbilts Cornelius Vanderbilt made a huge fortune in railroad construction. When he died in 1877, he left his family $200 million. Family members used part of this money to build seven mansions on Millionaires' Row. New Yorkers were used to plain brownstone buildings. They were amazed to see the fancy limestone mansion built by Vanderbilt's son, William Vanderbilt. They thought it looked like a French castle.

Some houses on Millionaires' Row were made to look like castles.

The Carnegie mansion covered an entire city block.

The Carnegies In 1901, the richest man in the world was Andrew Carnegie. He had just sold his steel company for $300 million. For many years, Carnegie lived next door to the Vanderbilts. Later, he built a 64-room mansion that had amazing technology for its time. For example, a miner's cart ran back and forth on a track in the basement. The cart hauled the two tons of coal needed every winter day to keep the huge house warm.

Some of the older families of New York society did not like these new millionaires and their flashy ways. The "old rich"—those who had been rich for a long time—called the mansions of the "new rich" tacky. It was vulgar, they said, to show off one's wealth.

Amazing Mansions

During the Gilded Age, mansions arose everywhere that millionaires lived, worked, and played. They sprang up in places such as the Midwest, Florida, and North Carolina.

These were not America's first great homes. However, they were bigger and grander than earlier homes. They were more like European palaces. These mansions often had huge entrances that featured at least one grand stairway. The floors and walls were made of marble. Light poured in through stained glass windows and skylights. Expensive art was everywhere.

The Breakers in Newport, Rhode Island

The Music Room at the Breakers

A number of modern conveniences, such as indoor plumbing, first appeared in these homes. By the 1870s, central heating had made it possible to build those huge ballrooms and grand entrances. Candles were replaced first by gaslights and then, in the 1920s, by electric lights.

In the summer, many people left the cities for places such as Long Island, New York, or Newport, Rhode Island. In Newport, owners called their summer homes "cottages," but they were more like palaces. Newport's biggest cottage is The Breakers. Built by Cornelius Vanderbilt II in 1895, The Breakers needed about 50 servants to run the place. It has 70 rooms.

Cornelius Vanderbilt's younger brother William built Marble House in Newport as a birthday present for his wife, Alva. What a birthday present it was! It cost about $11 million to build, with $7 million spent just on marble.

More Mansions

These mansions were like palaces, but they were also homes. Today, many of them are museums. Guides at The Breakers tell stories about the Vanderbilt family, such as the time when one young girl had a fit of temper. She was so angry that she locked several adults inside one of those fancy rooms!

One Newport estate is more famous for what is outside than inside. Called Green Animals, this home has more than 80 pieces of topiary. Topiary art involves trimming trees and shrubs into shapes. In this garden, trees have been shaped to look like animals.

George Vanderbilt created Biltmore House, which remains the largest privately owned home in the United States. Located in the mountains of Asheville, North Carolina, it has 250 rooms and 65 fireplaces. The estate is designed to be self-supporting. It has its own farm to grow food and to raise cows and chickens.

Topiaries in the garden of Green Animals

Architect Richard Morris Hunt designed both The Breakers and Biltmore House.

Today, the Biltmore estate includes nearly 8,000 acres and more than 200 buildings. Thousands of tourists visit each year, trying to imagine what it would be like to live in such a place.

Just before work started on Biltmore House, George Vanderbilt traveled to England and France with his architect. They visited many country homes to get ideas for the new house. They also brought back furniture, paintings, and statues.

The real artists behind these mansions were the architects. Two of the Gilded Age's most famous architects were Stanford White and Richard Morris Hunt. Their work blended European and American styles in a new style known as American Renaissance. Hunt designed Biltmore House.

Giving Money Away

Some Gilded Age millionaires were interested only in spending their money on themselves. Others felt they owed something to society. They became philanthropists (fuh•LAN•thruh•pists), or people who believe in trying to help others. These people often give large amounts of money or time to special causes. John D. Rockefeller and Andrew Carnegie were famous not only for their wealth but also for the money they gave away.

Rockefeller, the world's first billionaire, helped found the University of Chicago, giving the school $35 million. He also created several foundations, including the Rockefeller Institute for Medical Research. By the time he died in 1937, he had given away $530 million.

Rockefeller and his son gave away much money. Rockefeller Center in New York City was named after the family.

One of many Carnegie public libraries

Andrew Carnegie made a huge fortune in the steel business. He often said, "The man who dies rich dies disgraced." He believed it was his duty to use his money to help others. By the time he died in 1919, he had given away $351 million.

Carnegie wanted everyone to have the chance for an education. He believed people could educate themselves if they had books. At the time, however, few towns had public libraries. Carnegie decided he would build a free library for any town that asked him. His corporation built 2,509 libraries around the world.

Carnegie also built Carnegie Hall. This great New York City building is one of the most famous concert halls in the world. Many of the world's greatest musicians have performed there.

Carnegie's Heroes

In 1904, Andrew Carnegie started the Carnegie Hero Fund. It honors citizens who risk their lives for others. Two men who died trying to rescue others in a mine explosion were the first to be honored. To date, more than 9,000 Carnegie Medals have been awarded.

Lessons from the Gilded Age

Reminders of the Gilded Age are everywhere. Thousands of people still tour its mansions. Many important public buildings, such as the New York Public Library, were built by Gilded Age millionaires.

Oprah Winfrey is a talk show host and philanthropist.

Every year *Forbes* magazine prints "the Forbes 400," a list of the 400 richest people in the United States. The idea has not changed since Caroline Astor kept track of her own 400.

Some believe that talk show host Oprah Winfrey is today's society leader. Her tastes help decide what is popular. Like the leaders of the Gilded Age, Winfrey has a lot of money, and like many of them, she gives money to hundreds of causes.

Bill Gates has traveled around the world to bring better health care to people in developing countries.

The biggest philanthropist today is Bill Gates, who started the Microsoft computer software company. With his wife, Melinda, he has started the Bill and Melinda Gates Foundation. Like Carnegie, Gates helps libraries. His foundation has paid to bring the Internet to thousands of public library computers. The foundation is also working to bring medicines and medical care to those in need around the world.

The founder of eBay, Pierre Omidyar, is also a philanthropist. Omidyar and his wife, Pam, have donated millions of dollars to organizations around the world. Recently, they created Omidyar Network. This website connects people with ideas on how to make the world a better place to others who have the means to help them.

Like Rockefeller and Carnegie, many wealthy families today have turned their attention from business to philanthropy. By spreading their wealth, they are helping people all over the world.

15

Think and Respond

1. What were some businesspeople called during the Gilded Age?

2. Who were "Mrs. Astor's 400"?

3. In what important way did Andrew Carnegie help many cities and small towns?

4. What are two things John D. Rockefeller and Andrew Carnegie had in common?

5. Why do you think some people donate their time and money to helping others?

 # Activity

Imagine that you are a philanthropist. Make a list of some ways in which you would like to help others. Share your list with the class.